Women Across the Globe
Frame-Worthy Coloring Book
in Light Gray Scale

ARGENTINA

ANGOLA

AUSTRALIA

BRAZIL

CANADA

CHINA

COLUMBIA

COSTA RICA

CROATIA

CUBA

DENMARK

EGYPT

GREECE

HAWAII

INDIA

INDONESIA

ITALY

JAPAN

KAZAHKSTAN

MALAYSIA

MEXICO

MOROCCO

NIGERIA

PAKISTAN

PERU

PHILIPPINES

PUERTO RICO

ROMANIA

RUSSIA

SOUTH KOREA

SPAIN

SWITZERLAND

TANZANIA

THAILAND

TURKIYE

UKRAINE

UNITED KINGDOM

UNITED STATES

VIETNAM